# Realm of Reverie

Devi Meenakshi Karthigeyan

BookLeaf Publishing

India | USA | UK

Presentation by *BookLeaf Publishing*

Web: www.bookleafpub.com

E-mail: info@bookleafpub.com

ISBN:9789363314115

First edition 2024

# DEDICATION

To my dearest mom and dad who ignite the
spark in me to dream...

# ACKNOWLEDGEMENT

First and foremost, I extend my deepest gratitude to the divine presence for guiding me through this journey and blessing me with the strength and resilience to persevere.
To my beloved parents, S.Karthigeyan and V.Umamageswari,  your unwavering love, encouragement, and sacrifices have been the foundation upon which I've built my dreams. I am endlessly grateful for your boundless support and unwavering belief in me.
To my cherished family, thank you for your understanding, and encouragement. Your love and encouragement have been a constant source of inspiration and motivation.
To my dear friends, your companionship, and laughter have enriched my life in countless ways. Thank you for being my pillars of strength and for always believing in me.
To my esteemed teachers and professors, your guidance, wisdom, and dedication to education have shaped my intellectual growth and ignited my passion for learning. I am indebted to your mentorship and grateful for the invaluable lessons you've imparted.

I am profoundly thankful to everyone who has played a role, big or small, in shaping this journey. Your kindness, support, and encouragement have been a beacon of light during challenging times.

# In the Shadows of Patriarchy: A Dream to Abolish

Strong is her desire, to take up engineering
*"Oh! Why strain yourself, while there is teaching"*
Preaches the crowd

She sheds her blood, sweat and tears to build a home
*"Oh! Immovable property is inherited only by sons"*,
Preaches the crowd

To explore the nook and corner of the world she
yearns
*"Oh! Travelling isn't for girls… We are here to
protect you!"*,
Preaches the crowd

As she is beaten over and over
Escaping reality seems her only solution…
*"Oh! Divorce will label you immoral"*,
Preaches the crowd

To end the patriarchy and inequality she voices
out…
*"Oh! A false feminist who is headstrong"*
Preaches the crowd!!!

# A Quest to Put an End to Body Shaming

You'll fly away if there is a storm
In gaining weight there is no harm

An elephant would look smaller near you
Lose pounds, at least a few

Why don't you try out that fairness cream
To marry a fair girl is every man's dream

Why don't you consult a dermatologist?
Curing pimples…added to the list

Wearing spectacles diminishes your allure
Get contacts instead, your future will be secure

These are a few of the many…
That people believe, makes her funny

But isn't she perfect the way she is?
When will this world ever comprehend this?

# Words of a Wanderlust

To traverse time zones
To get away from mobile phones
To delve into the depth of oceans
To embrace the constant motion
To enjoy the smile of a stranger
To gain wisdom from the stories they utter


To experience the beauty transcendentals yapped
about
To explore the streets that poets glorified about
To seek a novel perspective
To indulge in the culture's collective

To experience life and its beauty
By indulging in travel and its bounty.

# Whispers in the Dark

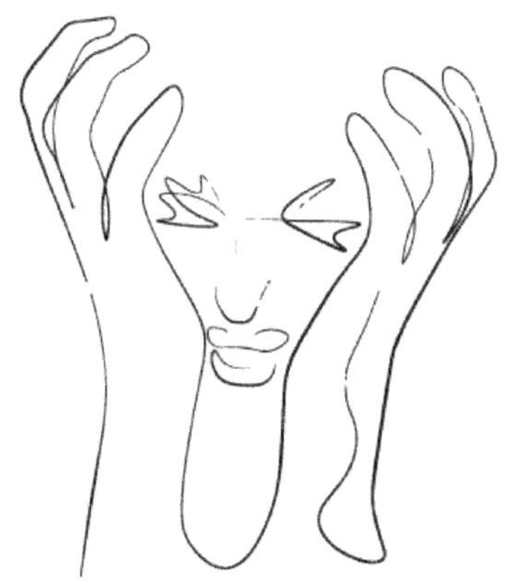

It's happening again,
Those voices in my brain
Eating every fiber of my being
Regardless, I'm expected to be gleeing

How do I escape these thoughts?
That's screaming to connect life's dots
Or worse, constantly pondering heavily,
If there are even any…

Seeking help seems to be the one way out
Oh! But the reluctance and self-doubt are stout.
SAVE ME!!! I want to scream
Would mental illness be addressed,
At least in my DREAMS???

# A Dream to be Seen

Hello? Hello? Hello?
I'm sinking in this world so shallow
I hope to be heard.
But considered not even one among the herd
I embellish myself longing to be looked at.
Time and again, I end up being hurt.

You mention me in your Instagram story.
As your sweetheart daring dearie.
Do you even know my tears and desire?
What you know is lesser than what a stranger
inquires!

Oh! I'm sinking in this world so shallow
Why has the standard of a bond sunk so low?

In this rat race that is wrapped in superficiality
All I long for is a touch of originality!!!

# Silent Storms

Little do they know that I want to shed tears
Little do they know that I am sinking with
responsibilities
Little do they know that I am capable of feeling
as well
Little do they know that I crumble under the
term 'Masculine'
Little do they know that I want to be cared for
Little do they know that I want to have deep
conversations
Little do they know that sports and gym do not
define me
Little do they know I am not a rock but just a
human!

# The Art of Letting Go

As memories roam to and fro
I ease my grip to let you go
Like the dandelion that floats in the gentle
breeze
All I want is for this moment to freeze.

Time whispers softly, it's time to part
Embrace the freedom, unchain the heart.
For in letting go, a brighter path might appear
But I can't stand the thought that you'll no
longer be near.

So I bid farewell to what was once mine.
With a heavy heart, I loathe life's design

Yet, with each goodbye, a new hello
I am slowly learning the art of letting go!!!

# Chasing the Truth

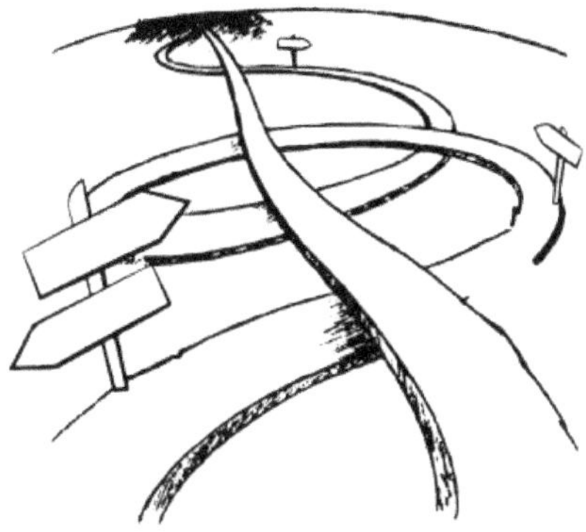

In the world so wide and questions deep
Where regrets lurk and secrets keep
I delve into the depths of thought
Where answers never seem caught

I suffocate in this whirl of questions and
directions
As I endlessly seek
For in the longing, this never-ending quest
Resides serenity, a silent unrest.

# Gentle Reverie

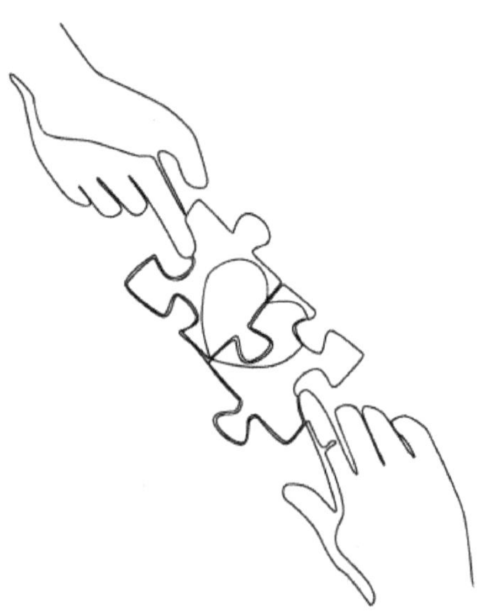

In the depth of darkness with hope
Where the whisper of eternity seems a
downward slope
I look for help to tape my broken pieces
And my shattered soul, before my time ceases

And then dawns a thought crystal clear
It is me who has to break that fear
The wounds of yesterday start to mend
As dreams of healing softly ascend.

Those broken pieces and shattered soul
I slowly patch back, to make me whole
Occasionally self doubts pertain
Pulling me down again

Yet I march forward without a frown
For healing is slow yet steady
And to rebuild and heal…
Yes, I am READY!!!

# A Plea...

Bomb Blasts! Bomb Blasts! Everywhere
Peace…. Nowhere
Where did we lose our humanity and unity?
To see the suffering lives is such a pity

Who gave us the right to take away someone's
life?
When would we come together to end this
pathetic life?
"All the world's a stage," says Shakespeare
In this short act, why do we have to live in fear?
Though storms may rage and tempest roar
I aspire for peace to finally soar!

# An Ode to Sisterhood

In laughter shared, tears embraced
Hugs so warm, scars erased
For the bond is immensely pure
I've never felt so secure.

Healing all those doubts and fear
You hold me close to your heart so dear
I finally unveil the beauty of sisterhood
As I feel 'heard and understood'!

In the gentle glow of twilight's hue
A dream of sisterhood pure and true

# Essence Unbound

The search is endless
No matter how hard I try
To comprehend, who am I?

Am I the memories of the past
Or all those decisions that never last

Am I a breeze at this moment?
The present?
But my choice doesn't seem to align
with other's intent.

Am I the pursuit?
The future?
Those endless possibilities, I can't possibly
measure.

Maybe I am a blend of these facets
Would I ever unravel this secret closet?

# Threads of Constraints

The institution which supposedly teaches gender equality
With the attire of the girl, judges her quality,
*"Don't wear your ponytail so high.*
*The swing and sway allures that guy."*

*"Make sure you cover up with a shawl"*
They perceive that, if not, the society would fall!

God forbid if she wears a skirt till her knee.
They label, that she does so only for people to see.
Can she ever dress just to feel beautiful

Without people burning down her character so
dreadful?
I yearn for them not to judge her by her dress
code
For within her heart, the truth's bestowed.

# Musings of the Soul

I dream to live life to the fullest
To discover the point of life
To experience butterflies yet feel at home
To be wrapped in respect and care
To fill the voids in my heart
To stumble and to be caught
To encounter moments where words would fail
To fall and rise in love
To speak words
To speak worlds!
Oh! I dream of living life to the fullest!!!

# Symphony of the Heart

As my yearning heart with dreams takes flight
Surpassing the sphere of left and right
I dream of a society that is tranquil and free
Where arts thrive with jubilant glee

No longer chained by rigid decree
Medicine and engineering are not the only key
But pathways wide, for hearts to implore
In the realms of art, we seek humanity's core

Painters brush the sky with hues untold
Sculptors mold dreams in forms bold
Writers weave tales, worlds unfurl
Musicians compose, and emotions swirl

In this realm of boundless creation
Arts embraced, without hesitation
For in diversity, true beauty lies
In every stroke, every note that flies

Like kids follow their hearts and decide
Breaking the stereotypes to learn for pride
Embracing the subjects where the soul is the
guide
Disregarding the soul-wrecking constraint to
abide

# Solace...

They say you are scary
They say you are imperfect
Leave you all alone.
While they are sound asleep…
Your very name depresses the crowd
I wish you could see I'm not one among them
They would never for a moment.
Comprehend the comfort I seek in you
Perceive the peace you provide
Fathom the way you hug my soul!
So, my dearest darkness…
Don't you ever feel forsaken
Behold me as I see you… for you!

Admire your beautifully flawed perfection
With my yearning eyes wide awake
Wanting nothing but you!

# Song of the Spirit

As the cold wind strikes her hair
Her solitary soul leans back
Seeking solace in Mother Nature's knack
Hoping that her heavy heart
The serenity would bear

Her yearning gaze falls on a lustrous bee
So did the wondrous creature's gaze on her
All her despondence seems to blur
Though venomous, at least fond though she

Disregarding her cynical, logical side
She finds her eyes glued to the venomous elf
The tiny brut springs her sharply like a celt
The very being she thought she could confide
Strangely, in a bewildered state
She found herself
Wondering if it was agony or exhilaration she
felt?!

# Flames of Fortitude

As she munched on that mouth-watering chocolate
"This is the reason you gain weight"
Said her husband with so much hate!
Facing a judgmental society was her unfortunate fate!

Drawn to the aroma from the kitchen
To enter and smell, she was neglected permission
Apparently, it is a sin*** 'Menstruation'
Her heart longed to banish the superstition!!

"Six!!! She exclaimed as she watched the
nail-biting match…
A sarcastic comment had the entire batch
"A girl admiring sports?" What a mismatch!
From such sexism, when will this society hatch?

Gazing at her book in the moonlight at peace
Her brother's screams and shouts shattered her
ease!
With every new day, the abuses increase…
Will this domestic violence ever cease?

Her friendly gentle fingers stroked his hair
Something dawned and she was suddenly
self-aware
She knew the public would object to it as … Not
Fair!!
Why does a 'Girl-Guy Friendship' cause such
despair?

A million are the problems she faces daily…
Yet with a strong heart, she marches bravely
Not fair is the day she'll be treated equally
Higher this phoenix will rise - I believe firmly.

# Threads of Us

Art in all its glory  is the essence of our daily
discussions
We delve into the depths of our creations and its
first impressions
You call me beautiful , not the way others blurt it
out superficially
Rather with intent making those words your very
own enchantingly
We spend hours speaking about the most
mundane things
Knowing it is in these moments the beauty of
life elegantly rings
We flood with tears trying to comprehend those
unintentional scars

With the spark of joy of being seen under the
moonlight and stars
It is in that moment when you recollect the
tiniest detail
I discern that you are to be weaved intricately in
my life's tale!

www.ingramcontent.com/pod-product-compliance
Lightning Source LLC
Chambersburg PA
CBHW071234140726
47996CB00007B/2606